Robert Quackenbush

WHAT HAS WILD TOM DONE NOW?!!!

A STORY OF THOMAS ALVA EDISON

•

Prentice-Hall, Inc.

ENGLEWOOD CLIFFS, NEW JERSEY

FOR PIET

Printed in the United States of America

Prentice-Hall International, Inc., London
Prentice-Hall of Australia, Pty. Ltd., North Sydney
Prentice-Hall of Canada, Ltd., Toronto
Prentice-Hall of India Private Ltd., New Delhi
Prentice-Hall of Japan, Inc., Tokyo
Prentice-Hall of Southeast Asia Pte. Ltd., Singapore
Whitehall Books Limited, Wellington, New Zealand

10 9 8 7 6 5 4 3 2 1

Library of Congress Cataloging in Publication Data

Quackenbush, Robert M.
  What has Wild Tom done now? A story of Thomas Edison

  SUMMARY: Humorous highlights of the life of the prolific
inventor who gave the world such useful items as the electric
light, motion pictures, and the phonograph.
  1. Edison, Thomas Alva, 1847-1931—Juvenile literature.
2. Inventors—United States—Biography—Juvenile literature.
[1. Edison, Thomas Alva, 1847-1931. 2. Inventors 3. Humor]
I. Title.
TK140.E3Q33   621.3′092′4 [B] [92]   80-26392
ISBN 0-13-952168-2

CONTENTS

Thomas Alva Edison, born in 1847, was the youngest of seven children. He was hard to manage and harder to understand. He was curious about everything—a born inventor. He was always into something like sitting on a nest of eggs to see if he could make them hatch or experimenting in the cellar with chemicals that might blow up.

2 TOM'S NARROW ESCAPES

Tom had many narrow escapes with his experiments and investigations. When looking to see how wheat was stored, he fell into a bin and was nearly buried in the grain. When exploring a bee's nest, he got butted by a ram. When building a bonfire behind a barn, away from the wind, he burned down the barn. But none of this—not even a public spanking for the barn fire—stopped Tom from being curious.

Tom went to school for all of three months. During that time, he was full of mischief. He caused an uproar when he caught a squawking chicken with a hook and line from the school window. He drew pictures at his desk when it was time to copy things from the board. He questioned everything that was said. All of this made the teacher angry. He did not believe that Tom was worth keeping in school. So Tom's mother, a former high school teacher, taught him his lessons at home. She succeeded in turning him into a rapid and eager reader.

When Tom was 12, he got a job as a newsboy on a train that traveled the short distance between his home town of Port Huron and Detroit, Michigan. Before his return trips, he had several hours of free time in Detroit. He would spend them in the library reading all kinds of books. Then he would go back to the train's baggage car, where he had set up a workshop, and do chemical experiments. One day some of the chemicals caught fire by accident and blew up. Tom wasn't hurt, but this ended his experiments on the train.

15

5 TOM TO THE RESCUE

By the time Tom was 15, he was a businessman. He owned a newspaper store and a vegetable store and he was hiring a newsboy for his train route. He was also printing his own newspaper. Then one day, Tom bravely rescued a station agent's baby son from the path of a runaway train. The agent was so grateful to Tom that he taught him how to send and receive telegraph messages. Tom became one of Western Union's fastest operators. Most of the money he earned went for books and equipment so he could keep on with his chemistry projects. But one of his experiments exploded in Port Huron's telegraph office and blew Tom out of a job. And so, at 16½, Tom went on the road.

Tom traveled from Ontario, Canada to New Orleans as a telegraph operator. But wherever he went, his experiments kept getting him into trouble and costing him many a job. In Louisville, for example, he spilled a bottle of acid, which seeped through the floor and put holes in the ceiling, furniture, and carpet of the office below. It was the manager's office! Once more, Tom was out of a job and his future did not seem promising.

7 TOM, THE MESSY DRESSER

From Louisville, Tom went to Boston to work for the Western Union office in that city. He arrived looking his worst. This was not unusual, because Tom was always a messy dresser. His clothes were always wrinkled and his hair was seldom, if ever, combed. His fellow workers in Boston, who wore neat suits, shirts, and ties, poked fun at the way Tom looked. Tom couldn't have cared less. His experiments were all that mattered to him. So, when he had saved enough money, he quit being a telegraph operator and set up a workshop in Boston. Now he could dress just as he pleased. For the next fifty years he wore a long white lab coat and a floppy straw hat that became his trademark.

8 TOM'S USELESS INVENTION

At the age of 21, Tom made his first invention—a voting machine. Using it, congressmen in Washington could instantly record "yes" and "no" votes at their meetings. Tom went to Washington and showed how his machine worked. But the congressmen were quick to tell him that it was the last thing on earth they wanted. They explained that they needed a delay in counting votes. It was often the only way they could stop unwanted laws. With that, Tom returned to Boston vowing never to invent anything that was not needed.

With the money, Tom set up a factory in Newark, New Jersey. There, he manufactured tickers and other electrical things and hired a team of outstanding men to help him to make his inventions. One of these was a telegraph that could send two messages and receive two messages at once. During this time, he fell in love and got married. Just after the wedding, he remembered something he had to do back at the laboratory. At midnight he was still there. He had forgotten all about his bride!

Tom wanted time to work on more inventions, but his factory took up too many hours. So he closed the factory and moved into a two-story building in Menlo Park, New Jersey. It became the first laboratory for industrial research, where many people worked at Tom's side doing experiments. Hundreds of inventions came from Menlo Park, including the microphone, the phonograph, and the electric light. Tom became known as the "Wizard of Menlo Park" and "Father of the Electrical Industry." Soon, he opened an even larger laboratory and factory in West Orange, New Jersey.

12 TOM MAKES MOVIES

Tom worked on problems that others had been unable to solve, and this led to some of his greatest successes. The electric light was one, though it took him two years and more than 1000 tries before he finally invented a bulb that could light. Another successful invention was moving pictures. Tom borrowed a little from this inventor, a little from that one, and put it all together into a long box with a peephole. This machine showed the world's first moving pictures. But Tom did not believe that movies would draw crowds. He was wrong, of course, and before long his West Orange plant also had a movie studio. Movie after movie was born there, including the first western called "The Great Train Robbery."

13 TOM'S LOST FORTUNE

While others made billions of dollars from Tom's ideas, he never got very rich from manufacturing and selling his inventions. This was because he put the money he earned back into his laboratory to spend on making new inventions, instead of looking for get-rich-quick business deals. But riches probably would not have changed the way Tom chose to live his 84 years. His only pleasures were being with his family and spending as many hours as possible in his laboratory. However, later in his life, something about him did change. Suddenly he began combing his hair and wearing suits that were neatly pressed. Which proves that people can accomplish anything when they are ready. Even so, Tom Edison's white lab coat and his earlier rumpled looks have remained the popular image of the scientist/inventor.

35

EPILOGUE:

WHAT THOMAS A. EDISON DID

No other person has ever made more inventions than Edison—a total of 1093. He invented the phonograph, light bulb, movies, and many more. He also made many improvements on the inventions of others, such as the telegraph, telephone, typewriter, and batteries. He invented a successful electric battery-powered automobile and he even experimented with flight. But of all Edison's inventions, the most outstanding were his laboratories at Menlo Park and West Orange. They were the world's first industrial research laboratories and the first of all modern research centers. When asked about all that he had done, Edison would quickly reply, "Anyone could do it. All they have to do is think!"